The Biggest Book of Reproducible Books

Student Books and Journals Provide Writing Opportunities that Encourage Children to Want to Write

by
Sherrill B. Flora

illustrated by
Timothy Irwin & Vanessa Countryman

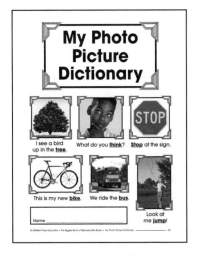

Publisher
Key Education Publishing Company, LLC
Minneapolis, Minnesota 55431

www.keyeducationpublishing.com

CONGRATULATIONS ON YOUR PURCHASE OF A KEY EDUCATION PRODUCT!

The editors at Key Education are former teachers who bring experience, enthusiasm, and quality to each and every product. Thousands of teachers have looked to the staff at Key Education for new and innovative resources to make their work more enjoyable and rewarding. Key Education is committed to developing and publishing educational materials that will assist teachers in building a strong and developmentally appropriate curriculum for young children.

PLAN FOR GREAT TEACHING EXPERIENCES WHEN YOU USE
EDUCATIONAL MATERIALS FROM KEY EDUCATION PUBLISHING COMPANY, LLC

Credits
Author: Sherrill B. Flora
Creative Director: Annette Hollister-Papp
Cover Design and Art: Peggy Jackson
Illustrator: Timothy Irwin & Vanessa Countryman
Editor: George C. Flora
Production: Key Education Staff

Key Education welcomes manuscripts and product ideas from teachers.
For a copy of our submission guidelines, please send a self-addressed, stamped envelope to:
Key Education Publishing Company, LLC
Acquisitions Department
9601 Newton Avenue South
Minneapolis, Minnesota 55431

Standard Book Number: 978-1-602680-38-8
The Biggest Book of Reproducible Books
Copyright © 2008 by Key Education Publishing Company, LLC
Minneapolis, Minnesota 55431

Printed in the USA · All rights reserved

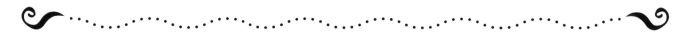

Contents

Introduction

Writing is an essential skill for effective communication. Children as early as preschool need to be in learning environments where they are able to explore a wide range of printed and written materials, and where they are encouraged to write frequently and for a variety of purposes. Teachers need to find many different ways to incorporate writing activities throughout the day, as well as keeping young children interested in learning how to write. *The Biggest Book of Reproducible Books* provides teachers and parents with reproducible books, journals, writing paper, activities, and ideas that will make "writing practice" both fun and motivating for young writers.

- **My Spelling Book** is a 35 half-page word book that is organized alphabetically with large easy-to-read word lists. This book can promote spelling, vocabulary development, and handwriting skills. This book is a writing resource — including 880 words and space for children to write additional words on each page. Activity ideas are also included as well as several pages of essential everyday words, such as colors, numbers, holiday words, and more.

- **My Photo Picture Dictionary** is a 44 page picture dictionary with 375 words, photo pictures, and sentences using each of the words. This is a tremendous book for young children who are just learning how to read and write as well as for English Language Learners (ELL) and children who are struggling in school.

- **My Journal** and **My Storybook** have a wide variety of reproducible writing paper and "design your own" covers. Teachers can choose the appropriate line width (kindergarten and primary widths), the number of lines and illustration boxes on each of the pages, and the number of pages in each journal or storybook for their individual students. Young children, or struggling writers, may only want pages with two writing lines, whereas older or more skilled children may wish to write full pages. A large list of journal topics, writing suggestions, story writing guidelines, and publishing ideas are also provided for the teacher.

- **My Phonics Book** can be as large as 76 half-pages, including over 2300 words organized by phonograms— long and short vowel sounds, beginning and final consonant blends, r-controlled vowels, beginning and ending consonant digraphs, and vowel digraphs and diphthongs. Children will add more pages to their phonics books as their skills grow. Blank lines are provided on each page for the children to write down additional words.

- **My "All About Me" Book** comes with 27 half-pages designed to encourage children to write and draw pictures about themselves and about topics that are personally important. This book is a fun "year-long" project, which should include many other pages and drawings created by the children during the year.

- **My Year Book** comes with 21 half-pages that help children write about school year memories, special events, friends, teachers, things they have learned, and how they have grown. This is another book that is fun to work on all year long. Writing about school parties, field trips, and other special events right after they have happened make the writing experiences much more valuable. Encourage the children to add their own pages. This book will become an individual special memory book for each child.

- **My Own Newspaper** offers teachers two different templates and a full page of detailed teaching suggestions for creating classroom newspapers as well as for using the newspaper as an effective teaching tool.

- **Graphic Novels,** or what many of us call comic books, can be used to motivate children to read and write. Children delight in using the style and look of graphic novels when they dream up characters, plots, dialogue, and illustrations. Included are activity ideas for this format to be used as a springboard for creative writing and there are four different reproducible comic and filmstrip writing and illustration pages.

- **Accordion Books** are great fun to make and they allow the writer to decide "how long" or "how short" to make their story. Complete directions, additional activity ideas, and reproducible pages are provided.

- **Themed Shape Books** are found in the final section of *The Biggest Book of Reproducible Books*. The shape books encourage different types of story genres and a variety of reasons to write, such as journaling about a vacation, writing nonfiction information about a pet, a make-believe bedtime story, or a story written as science fiction.

The Biggest Book of Reproducible Books will provide a classroom of eager (and some not-so-eager) young writers with a wealth of materials, writing books, journals, suggestions, activities, and ideas that will encourage them to write about topics of interest. It will also help them to develop an understanding of the writing process and to practice some of the strategies needed to become good writers.

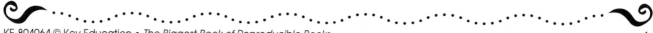

My Spelling Book

Name _____

My Spelling Book Activity Suggestions

My Spelling Book is meant to be used as a dictionary. The pages are organized alphabetically and contain over 880 high-frequency words, sight words, and common words that young children are learning to read and write. Space has been provided on each of the pages for children to write down additional new words.

How to Make My Spelling Book: Provide the children with copies of the entire book (pages 5A through 22). Cut along the dotted lines, punch two holes on the left side of each page, and bind the pages together using yarn or brads. Let the children design and color their own covers. The book will be printed one-sided. Encourage the children to use the back of each page to practice writing words that they find challenging.

Find-the-Page Race: Go though the pages of My Spelling Book with the class. Talk about how the pages are organized alphabetically. Play "find-the-page" race to help them become more familiar with alphabetizing. The teacher says the name of a letter, such as "M," and then the children, as fast as they can, find the "M" page. They should raise their hands once they have found the requested page.

Important Words: Talk about the last seven pages of the book that are titled "Important Words." Discuss how these pages are filled with many words that the children will need to use when writing. It will be very helpful to know where to locate these words.

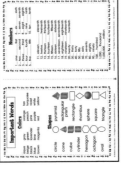

An Extra Blank Page: An extra blank page has been included on page 22A. If any of the children fill up an entire page, the blank page can be reproduced and added behind that page.

Aa

a	after	also	another
able	again	always	answer
about	age	am	any
above	air	among	apple
across	airplane	amount	are
act	all	an	around
add	almost	and	as
afraid	alone	animal	asleep
			ask
			at
			ate
			away

Bb

baby	because	better	boat
back	bed	between	both
bake	been	big	box
ball	before	bike	boy
bank	bell	bird	bread
be	below	birthday	bring
bear	beside	black	brother
beautiful	best	blue	brown
			build
			but
			buy
			by

Cc

cake	circle
call	city
came	class
camp	clean
can	clock
candy	close
cannot	coat
car	color

cook
corn
cow
cold
come
coming
could
count
crayon
cried
cry
cut

Dd

dad	did
dance	dig
danger	different
dark	difficult
date	dime
day	dinner
dear	dirty
deep	do

does
dog
dollar
don't
down
done
dog
doll

door
down
draw
dream
dress
drink
drive
drop
drum
dry
duck
during

Ff

fall
family
far
farm
farmer
fast
father
fear

feel
feet
few
find
fine
fire
first
fish

five
fix
flag
flew
floor
flower
fly
fold

follow
food
for
forest
found
four
friend
frog
from
full
fun
funny

Ee

each
ear
early
earn
earth
easel
east
easy

eat
eaten
eel
egg
eight
either
elephant
eleven

else
empty
end
enjoy
enough
enter
entrance
error

even
ever
every
exact
example
excellent
excite
exit
expect
explain
extra
eye

Gg

game giving gold gray
gap glad good great
garden glass good-bye green
gate glide got grew
gave glove grab group
get glue grade ground
girl go grand grow
give goes grass guard
guess
guest
guide
gum

Hh

had have hide hope
hair he high horse
hand head hill hot
happen hear him hour
happy heart his house
hard help hold how
has her home however
hat here hook hug
huge
hungry
hurry
hurt

Ii

I	inn	interest
ice	inner	into
ice cream	input	invent
icing	insect	invite
idea	inside	iron
if	instant	is
ill	instead	island
illness	instruct	it
important		itch
improve		item
in		its
inch		itself
include		
indoor		
information		
ink		

Jj

jab	jelly	jog
jack	jet	join
jacket	jewel	joint
jail	jewelry	joke
jar	jig	jolly
jaw	jiggle	jolt
jeans	jingle	journal
jeep	job	journey
		joy
		joyful
		judge
		jug
		juice
		juicy
		jump
		jungle
		junk
		jury
		just
		justice

Kk

kangaroo kick king
kazoo kickstand kiss
keep kid kit
kept kill kitchen
ketchup kin kite
kettle kind kitten
key kindness knee
keyboard kindly kneel

knew
knife
knit
knight
knob
knock
knot
know
knowing
knowledge
known
koala

Ll

land lead let
lake leaf letter
large learn library
last leave lie
late leaves life
laugh left lift
lay leg light
lazy less like

line
list
listen
little
live
long
look
loose
lost
lot
love
lunch

Mm

made
mail
make
man
many
map
march
mark

match
math
may
maybe
me
mean
men
middle

might
mile
milk
mind
mine
minute
mitten
money

month
moon
more
morning
most
mother
mouse
move
much
must
my
myself

Nn

nail
name
napkin
nation
nature
naughty
near
neat

neck
need
neighbor
neither
nest
net
never
new

next
nice
nickle
niece
night
nine
no
nobody

noise
none
noon
north
nose
not
note
nothing
noun
nowhere
number
nut

Oo

obey	office	only
object	often	onto
ocean	oh	open
octopus	oil	opening
odd	old	opposite
odor	on	or
of	once	orange
off	one	order

other	
ouch	
our	
out	
outside	
oval	
oven	
over	
owe	
owl	
own	
owner	

Pp

pack	part	picture
page	party	pie
paid	past	pig
paint	paste	pink
pair	pay	place
pal	pencil	plan
paper	people	plant
park	phone	play

please	
point	
police	
pour	
power	
practice	
pretty	
problem	
pull	
puppy	
push	
put	

Qq

quack	quart	queenly
quail	quarter	quench
quaint	quarterly	quest
quake	quarterback	question
quality	quartet	quibble
qualm	quartz	quick
quantity	queasy	quickly
quarrel	queen	quiet

quietly
quill
quilt
quintet
quip
quirk
quit
quite
quiz
quota
quotation
quote

Rr

rabbit	ready
race	real
radio	really
rain	reason
ran	receive
rattle	recess
reach	record
read	red

remember
remove
repeat
report
rest
return
rhyme
rich

ride
right
ring
river
road
robin
rocket
rode
room
round
ruler
run

S s

sad	see	should	sleep
said	seem	show	slow
same	seen	side	small
sat	sent	sight	snow
save	sentence	sing	so
saw	set	sister	some
say	she	sit	something
school	shoe	size	soon
			sound
			story
			street
			such

T t

table	thank	they	time
take	that	thing	to
talk	the	think	today
teacher	their	this	together
team	them	those	told
teeth	then	thought	tonight
tell	there	threw	too
than	these	through	tree
			tried
			true
			try
			turn

Uu

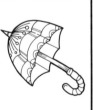

ugly
umbrella
unable
uncle
under
understand
understood
undid

undone
unfair
unhappy
unicorn
uniform
unit
unite
unjust

unkind
unknown
unless
unload
unlock
untie
until
unusual

up
upon
upper
upright
upset
upstairs
us
use
used
useful
usual
usually

Vv

vacant
vacation
vacuum
valentine
valley
value
van
vanilla

vanish
variety
vary
vase
vast
vegetable
vein
vent

verb
verse
version
very
vest
victory
video
view

visor
volunteer

village
vine
violet
violin
visit
visitor
volcano
volume
vote
vowel

Ww

walk   way   what   win
wall   we   when   wind
want   weather   where   window
warm   week   which   wish
was   well   while   with
wash   went   who   without
watch   were   why   woman
water   wet   will   won
word
work
would
write

Xx

x-ray
x-ray fish
xylophone

Zz

zany
zap
zebra
zero
zest
zig-zag
zillion
zip
zip code
zipper
zone
zoo
zoology
zoom
zucchini

Yy

yak
yam
yank
yap
yard
yardstick
yarn
yawn
yea
year
yearbook
yearly
yearn
yell
yellow
yelp
yes
yesterday
yet
yew
yield
yo-yo
yoga
yogurt
yoke
you
you'd
you'll
young
your
you're
yourself
yourselves
youth
you've
yummy

Numbers

1....one.........first	6....six..........sixth	
2....two.....second	7....seven...seventh	
3....three.......third	8....eight......eighth	
4....four......fourth	9....nine.......ninth	
5....five...........fifth	10...ten..........tenth	

11...eleven.............eleventh
12...twelve..............twelfth
13...thirteen...........thirteenth
14...fourteen.........fourteenth
15...fifteen.............fifteenth
16...sixteen............sixteenth
17...seventeen...seventeenth
18...eighteen.......eighteenth
19...nineteen.......nineteenth
20...twenty..........twentieth
30....thirty
40....forty
50....fifty
60....sixty
70....seventy
80....eighty
90....ninety
100....one hundred
1,000......one thousand
1,000,000......one million

Important Words

Colors

aqua	gray	orange	tan
beige	green	peach	turquoise
black	lavender	pink	violet
blue	lime	purple	white
brown	magenta	red	yellow

Shapes

circle

cone

cube

cylinder

hexagon

octagon

oval

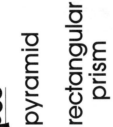

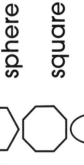
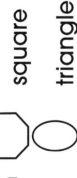

pyramid

rectangular prism

rectangle

rhombus

sphere

square

triangle

Holidays and Celebrations

New Year's Day, January 1.

Martin Luther King Day, third Monday in January.

Groundhog Day, February 2.

Lincoln's Birthday, February 12.

Valentine's Day, February 14.

President's Day, third Monday in February.

St. Patrick's Day, March 17.

April Fools's Day, April 1.

Earth Day, April 22.

Arbor Day is often the last Friday in April.

Mothers' Day, second Sunday in May.

Armed Forces Day, third Saturday in May.

Memorial Day, last Monday in May.

Flag Day, June 14th.

Fathers' Day, third Sunday in June.

Independence Day, July 4.

Parents' Day, fourth Sunday in July.

Labor Day, first Monday in September.

Grandparents' Day, Sunday after Labor Day.

Ramadan, varies yearly during the autumn season.

Columbus Day, second Monday in October.

Election Day, Tuesday on or after November 2.

Veterans Day, November 11.

Halloween, October 31.

Thanksgiving Day, fourth Thursday in November.

Christmas Day, December 25.

Days of the Week

Sunday .... Sun.

Monday .... Mon.

Tuesday .... Tues.

Wednesday .... Wed.

Thursday .... Thurs.

Friday .... Fri.

Saturday .... Sat.

Months of the Year

January .... Jan.

February .... Feb.

March .... Mar.

April .... Apr.

May .... May

June .... June

July .... July

August .... Aug.

September .... Sept.

October .... Oct.

November .... Nov.

December .... Dec.

Opposites

above	below	left	right
awake	asleep	long	short
back	front	lost	found
good	bad	loud	soft
before	after	love	hate
big	little	man	woman
black	white	more	less
bottom	top	mother	father
boy	girl	near	far
buy	sell	new	old
clean	dirty	no	yes
close	open	over	under
cold	hot	play	work
cry	laugh	poor	rich
day	night	pretty	ugly
easy	hard	push	pull
evil	good	right	wrong
fail	pass	same	different
fast	slow	she	he
follow	lead	sit	stand
friend	enemy	stop	go
funny	sad	take	give
full	empty	thin	thick
go	come	tidy	messy
hard	soft	true	false
head	foot	up	down
in	out	wet	dry
first	last	win	lose

Contractions

are not	aren't	she would	she'd
can not	can't	should not	shouldn't
could not	couldn't	that is	that's
did not	didn't	that will	that'll
do not	don't	there is	there's
does not	doesn't	they are	they're
had not	hadn't	they have	they've
has not	hasn't	they will	they'll
have not	haven't	they would	they'd
I am	I'm	was not	wasn't
I have	I've	we are	we're
I will	I'll	we have	we've
I would	I'd	we will	we'll
is not	isn't	we would	we'd
it is	it's	were not	weren't
it will	it'll	what is	what's
he is	he's	who are	who're
he will	he'll	who will	who'll
he would	he'd	who is	who's
here is	here's	will not	won't
let us	let's	would not	wouldn't
must not	mustn't	you are	you're
one is	one's	you will	you'll
she is	she's	you have	you've
she will	she'll	you would	you'd

extra spelling book page

Homophones

add......ad	made......maid
ant......aunt	marry......merry
ate......eight	meet......meat
bare......bear	need......knead
be......bee	new......knew
beat......beet	night......knight
been......bin	no......know
blue......blew	one......won
brake......break	or......ore
by......bye...buy	our......hour
brake......break	pair......pear
chilly......chili	plane......plain
close......clothes	pole......poll
dear......deer	rain......reign
die......dye	read......reed
do......due	red......read
doe......dough	right......write
fair......fare	road......rode
feat......feet	sale......sail
flower......flour	see......sea
for......four	seem......seam
great......grate	sell......cell
hair......hare	sent......cent
here......hear	shoe......shoo
hi......high	tea......tee
hole......whole	tide......tied
I......eye	vary......very
in......inn	weather...whether
led......lead	wood......would

My Photo Picture Dictionary
Activity Suggestions

My Photo Picture Dictionary is a 43 page picture dictionary with 375 words, photo pictures, and sentences. This is a tremendous book for young children who are just learning how to read and write, for English Language Learners, and for children who are struggling in school.

How to Make My Photo Picture Dictionary: Provide the children with copies of the entire book (pages 24 through 66). Punch three holes along the left side of each page and bind the pages together using yarn or brads. For added durability, have the children slip the pages into sheet protectors and then place all their dictionary pages into three-ring binders.

Encourage the Children to Add Pages to their Photo Picture Dictionaries: The best type of picture dictionary is one that is able to grow along with the child's vocabulary. The children can add pages to their photo picture dictionaries by using the reproducible blank dictionary page found on page 67. This page provides space for writing in four new words, adding an illustration (or photograph), and for using the word in a sentence. Children will delight in watching their dictionaries increase in size throughout the school year.

Learning to Alphabetize

- **Alphabet Necklaces:** Make 26 alphabet necklaces by punching a hole in the top of flash card alphabet letters and then stringing each flash card with a piece of yarn. Then have the children line up in alphabetical order wearing their letters.

- **Magnetic Letters:** Children love arranging magnetic letters. Place a magnetic board and magnetic letters in a learning center and let the children have fun lining up all the letters in alphabetical order.

- **Letter Stamps and Calculator Tape:** This is a favorite activity. Let the children have fun using letter stamps and calculator tape. They can stamp the letters in alphabetical order on the tape.

Dictionary Quiz Games

- **Find the Picture/Word-Version 1:** Each child should have a copy of My Photo Picture Dictionary. The teacher will say a word and then have the children try to find the word in their photo picture dictionaries.

- **Find the Picture/Word-Version 2:** Each child should have a copy of My Photo Picture Dictionary. The teacher will ask a question and then have the children try to find a word in their dictionaries that will answer the question.

- **Did I Spell it Right?** The teacher will spell a word and then have the children look up the word in their dictionaries to check if the teacher's spelling of the word was correct or incorrect. The teacher should spell some of the words incorrectly. The children will delight in finding that their teacher has spelled a word incorrectly.

- **Categories:** The children will each need a copy of My Photo Picture Dictionary, a pencil, and a piece of paper. The teacher says a category such as, "animals." The children will then look through their dictionaries and write down the names of all the animals they can find. Other categories that work well are clothes, transportation, feelings, food, school tools, people, and actions.

- **Find a Verb/Find a Noun:** The children will each need a copy of My Photo Picture Dictionary. Ask the children to look at a specific page or a specific letter. Have them make a list of the words on those pages that are nouns and a list of all those words that are verbs.

My Photo Picture Dictionary

I see a bird up in the **tree**.

What do you **think**?

Stop at the sign.

This is my new **bike**.

We ride the **bus**.

Look at me **jump**!

Name _____

Aa

a

This is **a** boy.

This is **a** picture of **a** boy.

again

Let's read the book **again**.

My mom read to me **again**.

alligator

Did you see the **alligator**?

am

I **am** a girl.

I **am** playing.

airplane

The **airplane** is flying.

Do you see the **airplane**?

and

He has a plane **and** a car.

He wants to play **and** play.

airport

I went to the **airport**.

I saw planes at the **airport**.

angry

He looks **angry**.

I think he is really **angry**.

answer

What is the **answer**?

Who knows the **answer**?

ask

She will **ask** me a question.

My teacher **asked** me a hard question.

ape

Is the chimp an **ape**?

asleep

She is **asleep**.

apple

The **apple** is red.

I like **apples**!

at

We are **at** school.

ate

Who **ate** the apple?

I **ate** it.

are

We **are** baking a cake.

These **are** my friends.

autumn

In **autumn** the leaves turn colors.

Bb

baby

The **baby** is happy.

bag

The **bag** is empty.

This is a **bag**.

ball

That **ball** is mine.

Playing with a **ball** is fun.

balloons

I have many **balloons**.

banana

I ate a **banana** for a snack.

bank

There is money in my piggy **bank**.

bat
I have a new **bat** and ball.

bath

I took a **bath** this morning.

bear

The **bear** lives in the forest.

bed

My **bed** is soft.

bee
Did the **bee** sting you?

bell

This is a school **bell**.

I hear a **bell** ringing.

big

This is a **big** animal.

bike

I can ride this **bike**.

Is your **bike** this big?

bird

A robin is a **bird**.

This **bird** can sing.

birthday

This is my **birthday** cake.

blocks

These are wood **blocks**.

Playing with **blocks** is fun.

boat

This **boat** can float.

I have a toy **boat**.

book

I have a favorite **book** to read.

Books are fun to read.

boy

I am a **boy**.

This **boy** is wearing a hat.

bus

I ride a **bus** to school.

Cc

cake

I think **cake** is my favorite food.

candy

Do you like to eat **candy**?

cap

This **cap** is new.

car

Can you drive a **car**?

My dad bought a new **car**.

carrot

The rabbit ate a **carrot**.

Carrots are good for you.

cat

My **cat** is the color orange.

Do you have a **cat**?

catch

He will **catch** the ball.

He is good at **catching** balls.

chair

Please, sit on our new **chair**.

This is a tall **chair**.

climb

Can he **climb**?

He is **climbing** up the wall.

cow

This is a **cow**.

Cows give us milk, butter, and ice cream.

clock

The **clock** tells us the correct time.

Is the **clock** ticking?

cold

The ice makes the drink **cold**.

crayon

May I use your red **crayon**?

I love new color **crayons**!

cry

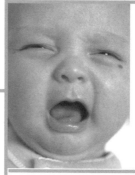

Did he **cry**?

Do you hear the baby **crying**?

color

He likes to **color**.

He is **coloring**.

cup

The **cup** is hot.

cookie

This is a chocolate chip **cookie**.

corn

I like to eat **corn** on the cob.

cut

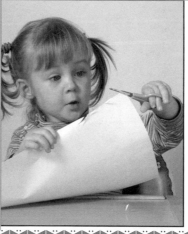

She is learning to **cut**.

She is **cutting** paper.

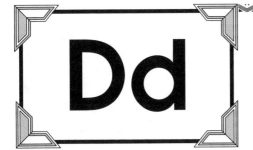

Dd

dad

I love my **dad**.

My **dad** plays with me.

day

What **day** should we go to the city?

desk

My mom has a new **desk**.

did

Did she get the candy?

dig

I like to **dig** in the sand.

She is **digging** with a shovel.

dime

This is a **dime**.

A **dime** is worth ten cents.

dish

I washed the **dish**.

The **dishes** are in the rack.

does

He **does** not want to go to sleep.

Does he have his pajamas on?

dog

My **dog** is my best friend!

dollar

I have a **dollar.**

A **dollar** is worth 100 cents.

doll

She has a new **doll**.

Many little girls like playing with **dolls**.

does

She **does** not want to get wet!

door

Open the **door**.

Who is knocking on the **door**?

down

He is going **down** the slide.

draw

What will she **draw**?

She is **drawing** a picture.

dress

This is a summer **dress**.

What **dress** should I wear to the party?

drink

I like to **drink** cold water.

Drinking water is good for you.

drum

I can play a **drum**.

This is a bass **drum**.

duck

Look at the **duck**.

Ee

easel

I paint on my **easel**.

We have many **easels** at my school.

eagle

This is an **eagle**.

The **eagle** is America's national bird.

easy

Skating is **easy** for me.

Is skating **easy** for you?

ear

I hear with my **ear**.

I have two **ears**.

early

Tonight I will go to bed **early**.

I have to get up **early** in the morning.

eat

What do you want to **eat**?

He is **eating** a sandwich.

Earth

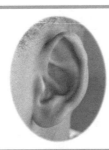

This is **Earth**.

We live on the planet **Earth**.

egg

I want an **egg** for breakfast.

We have a carton of **eggs** in our refrigerator.

elephant

This **elephant** has a long trunk.

Elephants are big animals.

empty

This basket is **empty**.

Did you **empty** the dishwasher?

end

At the **end** of the school day the children go home.

enjoy

These children **enjoy** school.

entrance

Go in the **entrance**.

The **entrance** sign is over the door.

equals

Five plus two **equals** seven.

exit

Go out the **exit**.

Look for the **exit** signs.

eye

This is an **eye**.

What color are your **eyes**?

F f

feather

Where did you find that **feather**?

family

This **family** has three children.

How many people are in your **family**?

feed

What will she **feed** the baby?

She is **feeding** the baby his dinner.

fan

Turn on the **fan**.

The **fan** will cool the room.

finger

Do not point your **finger**!

Each hand has five **fingers**.

farm

Have you ever been to a **farm**?

This **farm** has a barn.

fire

This **fire** truck moves fast!

This is a **fire** station.

father

The **father** pushes the stroller.

My **father** reads to me.

fish

I have a pet **fish** named Goldie.

Have you ever gone **fishing**?

flag

This is a **flag**!

There are many different types of **flags**.

fork

This is a **fork**.

Eat with a **fork**, not with your fingers.

flowers

These **flowers** are called tulips.

Flowers smell good.

fox

He is a sly **fox**.

The **fox** can run very fast.

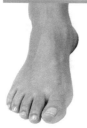

foot

This is a **foot**.

One **foot** plus one **foot** equals two feet.

friend

Are you my **friend**?

These children are good **friends**.

football

He is playing **football**.

Football is fun to watch.

frog

Jump like a **frog**.

Did you see that **frog**?

forest

A **forest** is full of trees.

Animals live in the **forest**.

funny

What's so **funny**?

That boy is very **funny**.

Gg

game

I have a new **game**.

Do you want to play a **game**?

gate

Open the **gate**.

The **gate** is closed.

get

He will **get** on the bus.

Let's **get** going!

gift

Did you buy the birthday **gift**?

I see many **gifts**.

giraffe

The **giraffe** is very tall.

Giraffes eat leaves from the tree tops.

girl

This **girl** is playing dress-up.

There are twelve **girls** in my class.

give

He will **give** her a gift.

He is **giving** her flowers.

glass

I want a **glass** of water.

Please put all the **glasses** on the table.

globe

I like looking at the **globe**.

The **globe** is a model of the Earth.

gorilla

Gorillas are huge animals!

This **gorilla** is called a silverback.

glue

Where is the **glue**?

I put my picture together with **glue**.

go

He has to **go**.

The bus **goes** back to the station.

He is **going** to school.

grape

I like to drink **grape** juice.

Grapes can be green or purple!

goat

This is a **goat**.

Goats like to eat a lot!

grate

Grate the cheese, please!

good

This is a **good** paper.

She did a very **good** job.

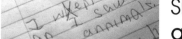

gum

Would you like some **gum**?

I like to chew **gum**.

Hh

hair

She has long **hair**.

Her **hair** is in a pony-tail.

have

I **have** many pumpkins.

Do you **have** a pumpkin?

hand

This is a baby's **hand**.

Her **hand** is little.

he

He is playing with marbles.

hang

Can you **hang** from the jungle gym?

She is **hanging**.

help

He likes to **help** his brother.

He **helps** his mom, too.

happy

She looks **happy**.

Why do you think she is **happy**?

hens

These **hens** can lay eggs.

hat

This looks like my grandma's **hat**.

hide

Please, do not **hide**.

The boy is **hiding** behind his hands.

hold

He will **hold** his dad's hand.

They are **holding** hands.

hour

Can you tell time on the **hour**?

horse

I want to ride a **horse**.

Horses can run very fast.

house

I live in a **house**.

Where is your **house**?

how

How far will the boy walk?

hose

Where is the garden **hose**?

hug

Do you **hug** your pet?

This boy is **hugging** his dog.

hospital

The ambulance drove to the **hospital**.

hot

I want to eat a **hot** dog.

Careful, the food is **hot**.

hurt

Is she **hurt**?

She **hurt** her knee.

I i

inside

The puppy is **inside** his house.

I

I can count on my fingers.

I am good at math.

iron

Careful, the **iron** is hot.

Do you like to **iron**?

ice cream

Who likes **ice cream**?

My favorite **ice cream** is vanilla.

is

He **is** doing his homework.

He **is** a good student.

in

They are going **in** the school bus.

ink

The **ink** is black.

it

It smells good.

Do you want to smell **it**?

J j

jello
I like cherry jello.

Jello with whip cream is good!

jacket
This is my new jacket.

jelly beans

Jelly beans are fun to eat.

jacks

I like the game of jacks.

jug
This is a water jug.

Fill the jug with lemonade.

janitor
This is our school's janitor.

The janitor works very hard.

juice
I love orange juice.

Do you like apple juice?

jeans

These are my blue jeans.

jump
I love to jump rope.

Look how high I can jump.

jeep
Have you ever ridden in a jeep?

K k

kangaroo

A baby **kangaroo** is called a joey.

Kangaroos jump very fast.

kazoo

Can you play a **kazoo**?

Kazoos are fun to play.

keep

I want to **keep** the turtle.

kettle

The tea **kettle** is whistling.

Someone put the **kettle** on!

keyboard

Can you play the **keyboard**?

The **keyboard** plays music.

keys

These are my dad's **keys**.

kick

She will **kick** the ball.

She **kicked** the ball into the net.

kind

She is very **kind**.

She treats her puppies with **kindness**.

king

He is the **king**.

Make way for the **king**!

kitten

Look at the cute **kitten**.

The **kitten** can climb trees.

kiss

She is giving him a **kiss**.

knee

Bend your **knee**.

I fell and hurt my **knee**.

kitchen

We cook in our **kitchen**.

It is your turn to clean the **kitchen**.

knew

She **knew** she would do well on the test.

She **knew** all the answers.

know

I **know** how to bake cookies.

He **knows** the answer.

kite

My **kite** flew very high!

How many **kites** are in the air?

koala

That little **koala** is up in the tree.

Koalas look very soft.

L l

ladybug

See the **ladybug**.

The **ladybug** is red and black.

lake

Let's go swim in the **lake**.

The **lake** looks very still today.

lamb

This is a **lamb**.

A **lamb** is a baby sheep.

lamp

Please, turn on the **lamp**.

Is that a new **lamp**?

large

This is a really **large** pumpkin.

laugh

It is fun to **laugh**.

leaf

Where did you find that **leaf**?

lemonade

I love **lemonade**.

The **lemonade** tastes good.

letter

Let's play with the alphabet **letter** blocks.

I can print all the **letters** in the alphabet.

library

The **library** is full of books.

lock

This is a **lock**.

Do you know how to open the **lock**?

like

I **like** baseball.

What do you **like** to play?

look

Look at what I see!

She is **looking** out the window.

lion

The **lion** is king of the beasts.
Lions run fast and roar loudly.

loud

He is **loud**!

Do you like **loud** music?

love

I **love** my cat.

My cat **loves** me, too.

listen

She likes to **listen** to music.

little

This is a **little** mouse.

lunch

What time do we eat **lunch**?

I have an apple in my **lunch**.

Mm

magnet

This is a **magnet**.

We learn about **magnets** in school.

make

Dad and I will **make** dinner.

We are **making** a salad.

man

This is a **man**.

My brother will grow up to be a **man**.

many

I have **many** blocks.

Do you have as **many** as I do?

map

This is an old **map**.

Maps are fun to study.

mask

This is a black **mask**.

Do you have a **mask** to wear to the party?

me

Look at **me**!

Can you come over to my house and play with **me**?

milk

I like to drink **milk**.

Do you like **milk**?

mine

This ball is <u>mine</u>.

This is <u>mine</u> and not yours.

mother

This is my <u>mother</u>.

My <u>mother</u> loves me very much.

mirror

Look in the <u>mirror</u>.

Can you see yourself in the <u>mirror</u>?

mouse

I just saw a <u>mouse</u>.

mittens

Where are my <u>mittens</u>?

<u>Mittens</u> keep your hands warm.

mouth

This <u>mouth</u> is smiling.

monkey

Here is a <u>monkey</u>.

<u>Monkeys</u> like to eat bananas.

mug

This is a tin <u>mug</u>.

moon

Can you see the man in the <u>moon</u>?

my

Here is a picture of <u>my</u> family.

<u>My</u> family is having a picnic.

Nn

nickle
This is a **nickle**.

A **nickle** is worth five cents.

name
What is your **name**?

My **name** is Mary.

night
It is dark at **night**.

nest
There are three eggs in the **nest**.

no
This sign means **no** walking.

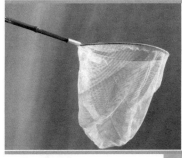

net
This is a butterfly **net**.

nose
My **nose** helps me to smell.

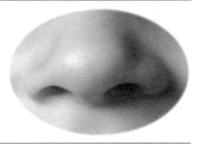

new
These are **new** baby shoes.

not
She does **not** want to go to bed.

She is **not** happy.

next
The puppy is sitting **next** to his house.

numbers
These are **numbers**.

I see eleven **numbers**.

Oo

one

This is a **one** way sign.

o'clock

It is three **o'clock**.

open

The book is **open**.

oranges

These are juicy **oranges**.

off

The receiver is **off** the phone.

out

He is getting **out** of the bus.

old

Do you think this lady is **old**?

My grandpa is getting **old**.

over

The puppy is jumping **over** his house.

on

The puppy is **on** top of his house.

owl

This is an **owl**.

The **owl** is in the tree.

P p

pear

Which **pear** do you want?

There are four **pears**.

pail

This **pail** is full of water.

I took the **pail** to the beach.

peek

I am going to **peek** around the corner.

I am **peeking** from behind the chair.

paint

I like to **paint**.

I will give this **painting** to my friend.

pencil

I have a new **pencil**.

I like colored **pencils.**

pan

Please wash the **pan**.

Where is the frying **pan**?

penny

This is a **penny**.

A **penny** is worth one cent.

panda

He is a black and white **panda**.

pen

This **pen** has blue ink.

My teacher uses a red **pen**.

paper

I use lined **paper**.

This is writing **paper**.

pet

She has a **pet** goat.

She is **petting** the goat.

please

She is signing, "**please**."

Please come here!

picture

This is a **picture** of some flowers.

I like the **picture**.

police

This is a **police** car.

Police help everyone.

pie

My mom made an apple **pie**.

popcorn

It is fun to make **popcorn**.

pig

I want a baby **pig**.

Here are two **pigs**.

pull

Both of us will **pull** the rope.

pizza

Who wants **pizza** for dinner?

puppy

This is my **puppy**.

We just call him, "**puppy**."

play

Do you want to **play**?

He is **playing** in his room.

put

I will **put** away the dishes.

Put the plate on the shelf.

Qq

quail

A **quail** is a pretty bird.

Quail live in the forest.

queen

The **queen** is wearing a beautiful dress.

The **queen** lives in a castle.

quarter

This is a **quarter**.

A **quarter** is worth twenty-five cents.

quiet

"Shhh," means to be **quiet**.

Please be **quiet**.

R r

rainbow

rabbit

Here is a **rabbit**.

Rabbits can hop very fast.

Look at the beautiful **rainbow**.

How many colors are in a **rainbow**?

raccoon

He is a **raccoon**.

The **raccoon** is trying to hide.

rake

She likes to use a **rake**.

Raking leaves can be hard work.

rain

read

She likes to **read** in bed.

Reading is her favorite thing to do.

restroom

This is a **restroom** sign.

Where is the **restroom**?

The girl is outside in the **rain**.

The **rain** is getting her wet.

ride

She likes to **ride** her horse.

She goes **riding** everyday.

She **rides** all around her ranch.

rock

I have a **rock** collection.

Here are many **rocks**.

roll

Can you **roll** the cookie dough?

This is a **rolling** pin.

ring

This is a big **ring**.

Do you like to wear **rings**?

rug

Wipe your feet on the **rug**.

I need to shake the **rug**.

river

This is a rocky **river**.

We skip rocks on the **river**.

ruler

This is a **ruler**.

A **ruler** has twelve inches.

robot

I have a toy **robot**.

My **robot** can walk and talk.

run

He sure can **run** fast.

He goes **running** everyday.

S s

shoes

These are running **shoes**.

My **shoes** are new.

sad

She looks **sad**.

Why do you think she is **sad**?

sit

Please **sit** down.

The little girl is **sitting** quietly.

said

When she answered the phone, she **said**, "Hello."

I **said**, "please get the phone."

saw

I **saw** a seal at the zoo.

skip

Do you know how to **skip**?

Skipping is fun!

She **skipped** home.

sleep

Did you **sleep**?

She is **sleeping** now.

school

I like going to **school**.

see

I **see** a bunny in a basket.

slide

He likes to **slide**.

Sliding is a lot of fun.

snow

I like to play in the **snow**.

Snow is cold.

street

This is a **street**.

I see a car on the **street**.

socks

Where are my **socks**?

I will put on my **socks**.

summer

We go to the beach in the **summer**.

stand

She can **stand** on her hands.

Please **stand** still.

swim

I like to **swim**.

She loves to go **swimming**.

star

This is a **star** cookie cutter.

There are many **stars** in the sky.

sun

The **sun** is hot.

It is a **sunny** day.

stop

This is a **stop** sign.

A **stop** sign is shaped like an octagon.

swing

She likes to **swing**.

She is **swinging**.

T t

television

Do you want to watch **television**?

table

This is a **table**.

It is a wood **table**.

the

The little girl is reading a book.

talk

She likes to **talk**.

She is **talking** on the phone.

there

There is a goat.

There is some goat food.

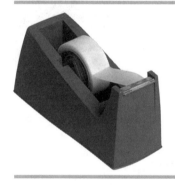

tape

Where is the **tape**?

I need some **tape**.

they

They are good friends.

What are **they** doing?

teacher

My **teacher** is nice.

Who is your **teacher**?

telephone

The **telephone** is ringing.

think

She likes to **think**.

She **thinks** a lot!

What could she be **thinking**?

this

This is a lot of fun!

Jump like this.

toy

Look, there is a toy box.

The toy box is filled with toys.

three

There are three blocks.

train

This is a wooden train set.

tiger

Look at the tiger.

Tigers have black stripes.

tree

There is a big tree.

That tree is full of leaves.

together

Let's play together.

triangle

This is a triangle.

A triangle has three sides.

too

She has too many books.

truck

I want a toy truck.

It is a dump truck.

top

A top is a fun toy.

The top spins.

turtle

I have a pet turtle.

Do you like turtles?

Uu

umbrella

We need an **umbrella**.

Get out the **umbrella**.

unicycle

I know how to ride a **unicycle**.

A **unicycle** has only one wheel.

uncle

My **uncle** is so much fun!

My **uncle** takes me to the park.

up

He is sitting **up** high.

He climbed **up** the hill.

upset

He looks **upset**.

Why do you think he is **upset**?

under

The puppy is **under** his house.

us

Look at **us**!

Come and play with **us.**

underwear

This is **underwear**.

Everyone wears **underwear.**

use

I get to **use** the new computer.

Vv

very

We can run **very** fast.

We are **very** good runners.

vacuum

Can I use the **vacuum**?

vest

This is a **vest**.

A **vest** can keep you warm.

valentine

I made you a **valentine**.

Happy **Valentine's** Day.

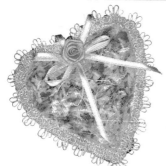

van

My dad got a new **van**.

veterinarian

When I grow up I want to be a **veterinarian**.

Veterinarians take good care of animals.

vase

Put the flowers in the **vase**.

Is that a new **vase**?

violin

I can play the **violin**.

vegetable

I planted a **vegetable** garden.

vulture

A **vulture** is a bird.

Vultures are large.

Ww

wagon

I have a red **wagon**.

Let's go for a ride in my **wagon**.

walk

We **walk** home from school.

Let's go for a **walk**.

wallet

The money is in my **wallet**.

want

I **want** to go fishing.

Do you **want** to go fishing?

wash

Please go and **wash** your hands.

I **washed** my hands.

watch

A **watch** tells you the time.

water

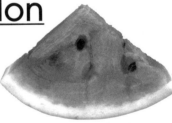

Let's drink some ice **water**.

The **water** is very cold.

watermelon

Watermelon is fun to eat.

we

We are great friends!

wet

He is getting very **wet**.

It is fun to get **wet**.

winter

The season is **winter**.

The **winter** months are cold.

what

What are you working on?

What do you want to do?

wolf

A **wolf** is a beautiful animal.

The **wolf** is howling.

who

Who will win?

Who wants to play soccer?

woman

My mom is a **woman**.

My little sister will grow up to be a **woman**.

wind

There is a lot of **wind** today.

It is a **windy** day.

worry

Do you **worry**?

He looks very **worried**.

window

Open the **window**.

Can you close the **window**?

write

He is going to **write** a story.

I am **writing** about a game.

X-ray

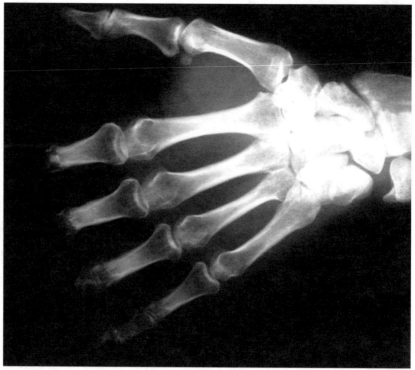

This is an **x-ray** of a hand.

Have you ever had an **x-ray** taken?

xylophone

Can you play a **xylophone**?

I have always wanted a **xylophone**.

Yy

yield

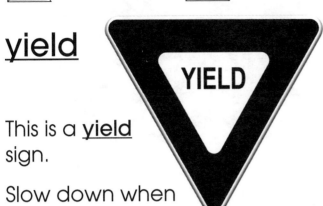

YIELD

This is a **yield** sign.

Slow down when you see a **yield** sign.

yo-yo

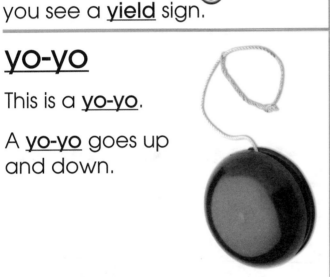

This is a **yo-yo**.

A **yo-yo** goes up and down.

yogurt

Fat Free

Do you like **yogurt**?

Yogurt is one of my favorite foods.

you

She is pointing at **you**.

Do **you** like to read and write?

young

He is **young**.

My grandmother acts very **young**.

yum

Yum, this ice cream is so good!

I think all ice cream is **yummy**.

Zz

zebra

A **zebra** looks like a horse.

Zebras have black and white stripes.

zigzag

Can you draw a **zigzag** line?

He **zigzaged** as he ran.

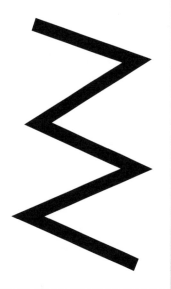

zip

Zip up your jacket before you go outside.

She is **zipping** up her sweater.

zoo

To get to the **zoo** just follow the sign.

What kinds of animals do you think we will see at the **zoo**?

(new word)

(new word)

(new word in a sentence)

(new word in a sentence)

(new word)

(new word)

(new word in a sentence)

(new word in a sentence)

My Journal and My Storybook
Activity Suggestions

How to Make My Journal or My Storybook: My Journal and My Storybook come with a wide variety of reproducible writing paper (pages 71–80) and "design your own" covers (pages 69–70). Teachers can choose the appropriate line width (kindergarten and primary widths), the number of lines per page, the size of the illustration boxes, as well as the number of pages put in each of the children's journals or storybooks. Young children or struggling writers may only want a couple of pages with two writing lines, where older or more skilled children may want journals filled with many pages and will be able to write full pages. Using the reproducible pages included in *The Biggest Book of Reproducible Books,* teachers are able to design developmentally-appropriate journals or storybooks for each of their students. Copy the pages and covers for individual students, punch holes along the left side of the paper, and bind the pages together with yarn or brads. The pages may also be stapled together.

My Journal Activity Suggestions

Journal Prompts: Provide the children with various journal prompts to help them get started writing. Add praise and positive comments to what the children have written. Remember, the purpose of journal writing is to provide meaningful writing practice using topics that interest and motivate young writers. Here are some ideas:

- The happiest time of my life . . .
- One question I would like to ask . . .
- If I could live anywhere it would be . . .
- The scariest dream I ever had . . .
- If I had a million dollars, I would . . .
- I think this rule is unfair because . . .
- My greatest adventure ever was . . .
- I knew the seed was magic when . . .
- This is my favorite sandwich . . .
- I am the happiest when . . .
- Look what lives in outer space . . .
- I want to tell you about my friend . . .
- The biggest mess I ever made . . .
- I like being a boy/girl because . . .

- I wish that I could . . .
- When I turn 16 years old . . .
- I very much dislike . . .
- My hero is . . .
- The worst thing ever . . .
- When I grow up . . .
- I see bugs everywhere . . .
- I would like to make . . .
- I saw a dinosaur in my . . .
- I get upset when . . .
- My favorite memory is . . .
- I do not like to . . .
- The magic wand . . .
- It really scares me when . . .

- My future wife/husband . . .
- My favorite story is . . .
- What really bothers me . . .
- My heart beats faster when . . .
- If I could fly, I would travel to . . .
- My toys can talk . . .
- The biggest thing I ever saw . . .
- This summer I want to . . .
- If I had a superhero power . . .
- I saw a very strange. . .
- I really don't like this food . . .
- I would pack in my suitcase . . .
- This weekend I am going to . . .
- If I had a camera, I would . . .

My Storybook Activity Suggestions

With these simple guidelines you can help young children learn how to write their own stories:

1. **Planning:** Teach them to use a simple graphic organizer of four boxes. One box is for the setting of their story; box 2 is for the characters; box three is for the problem; and box four is for the solution to the problem. Ask the children to write a few words in each of the boxes.

2. **First Simple Draft:** Have the children write a simple first draft. They should not worry about anything other than getting down their ideas.

3. **Conferencing with the Students:** During the first two sections the teacher should conference with each child. Ask questions and guide the children into clarifying the details of their stories.

4. **Revising and Editing:** This should be a combined effort between the teacher and the student. Provide dictionaries and word walls for spelling corrections, and also discuss parts of the story that may not make sense.

5. **Final Written Copy:** When the story seems to make good sense and the child has spelled all the words correctly, it is time to rewrite the story on the storybook pages as neatly as possible.

6. **Illustrations:** The last and final step is to illustrate the story in the boxes provided on each page.

My Journal

Name_____

My Storybook

The title of my story is:

_____

Name _____

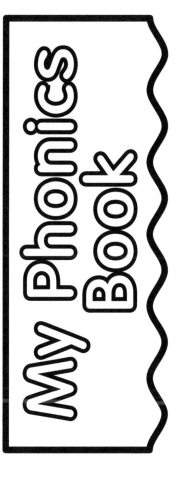

My Phonics Book

Name _____

✂

My Phonics Book
Activity Suggestions

My Phonics Book (pages 81A–119A) includes over 2300 words that are organized by phonograms, including the following: long and short vowel sounds, beginning and final consonant blends, r-controlled vowels, beginning and ending consonant digraphs, and vowel digraphs and diphthongs. Blank lines are provided on each page for the children to write in additional words.

How to Make My Phonics Book: Provide the children with copies of the entire book (pages 81A–119A). Cut along the dotted lines, punch two holes on the left side of each page, and bind the pages together using yarn or brads.

Let the children design and color their own covers. The book will be printed one-sided. Encourage the children to use the back of each page to practice writing words that they find to be challenging.

Adding Extra Pages: If any of the children fill up an entire page in their phonics books they can add extra pages by reproducing page 22A.

Introducing the Pages: My Phonics Book should not be presented all at once to the students. This book is meant to be introduced one page at a time. Provide the students with specific pages each time you introduce a new phonogram to the students. For example, when you introduce the beginning consonant blends "br–" you would give the students page 88 to add to their phonics books.

My Phonics Book Contents

a

act	cab	grass	pants
add	cat	had	panda
apple	class	ham	raft
as	crab	happy	rag
back	dad	has	sad
bad	fan	Jack	sang
band	fast	jam	stamp
black	flag	lamb	tack
		lamp	tan
		man	thank
		map	wag

e

bed
bell
best
cent
chest
den
dress
egg

end
fed
Fred
gem
get
head
hen
jet

Ken
led
lend
let
men
mend
met
Ned
nest
net
peg

pet
red
rent
rest
set
sled
spell
tell
ten
vet
went

i

bib
big
bill
chin
city
crib
did
dig

drink
fig
fish
gift
give
grin
him
hint

in
it
jig
Jim
kid
king
kiss
lick
lips
milk
mint

pick
pig
pin
ring
rink
sing
sit
thin
think
will
with

o

block	dot	knob	plop
Bob	frog	knock	rock
box	fox	lock	rob
cob	got	log	shop
cloth	hop	long	sob
crop	hot	mom	sock
dog	job	mop	spot
doll	Jon	not	stop
		ox	Tom
		pop	top
		pot	tot

u

bug	duck	hug	pump
bump	dunk	hum	rub
bus	fluff	hunt	rug
but	funny	jug	run
cub	fuzz	jump	sum
cup	gum	just	sun
cut	gush	luck	sung
drum	hub	mug	tug
		plug	truck
		puff	under
		pug	up

cl-

clack	Clara	clean
claim	clarinet	clear
clam	Clark	cleat
clamp	clash	clef
clan	clasp	clerk
clang	class	click
clank	claw	cliff
clap	clay	climb
		cling
		clinic
		clink

clip
clock
clog
close
closet
cloth
clothes
cloud
clown
club
cluck

KE-804064 © Key Education • The Biggest Book of Reproducible Books • My Phonics Book   -85A-

bl-

black	blink
blade	blip
Blake	blizzard
blame	bloat
bland	blob
blank	block
blanket	blond
blast	blood
blaze	bloom
bleach	blossom
bleed	blot
blend	blouse
bless	blow
blew	blubber
blimp	blue
blind	bluebells
	bluebird
	bluegill
	bluff
	blunt
	blur
	blurry

KE-804064 © Key Education • The Biggest Book of Reproducible Books • My Phonics Book   -85-

fl-

flag	flash
flagpole	flat
flake	flavor
flame	flaw
flank	flea
flap	fled
flapjack	flee
flare	fleet

flex	flop
flick	floss
flight	flour
fling	flower
flint	flu
flip	fluff
Flo	fluid
float	flurry
flock	flush
flood	flute
floor	fly

gl-

glad	glasses
gladly	glaze
glade	gleam
glance	glee
gland	gleeful
Gladys	glen
glare	Glenn
glass	glib

glide	gloom
glider	gloomy
glimmer	glory
glimpse	gloss
glisten	glove
glitch	glow
glitter	glowworm
gloat	glue
glob	glum
global	glut
globe	glutton

sl-

slab	slice	slit
slacks	slick	sliver
slam	slid	slope
slang	slide	sloppy
slant	slight	slosh
slap	slim	slot
slate	slime	slow
sled	sling	slug
sled dog	slip	slumber
sleek	slippers	slush
sleep	slippery	sly
sleepy		
sleet		
sleeve		
sleigh		
slept		

pl-

place	pleat	plum
plaid	pledge	plumber
plain	plenty	plume
plan	pliant	plump
plane	pliers	plunge
planet	plod	plunk
plank	plop	plural
plant	plot	plus
plaster	plow	plush
plastic	pluck	Pluto
plate	plug	Plymouth
platoon		
play		
playful		
plea		
please		

cr–

crab	crane	creep	crop
crack	crash	crest	cross
crackle	crate	crew	crow
cradle	crawl	crib	crowd
crafts	crayon	crick	crown
Craig	creak	cricket	crumb
cramp	cream	crime	crunch
crank	creek	crisp	crush
		critter	crust
		croak	crutch
		crock	cry

br–

brace	branch	breath	bring
bracelet	brand	breeze	brisk
brad	brass	brew	broil
brag	brave	bribe	broke
braid	bray	brick	brook
brain	bread	bride	broom
brake	break	bridge	broth
bran	breakfast	brief	brother
		bright	brow
		brim	brown
		brine	brush

dr–

drab	drape
draft	drastic
drag	draw
dragon	drawer
drain	drawing
drake	drawn
drama	dread
drank	dream

dreary	drive
drench	drizzle
dress	drone
dresser	drool
drew	droop
dribble	drop
dried	drove
drift	drown
drill	drum
drink	dry
drip	drying

fr–

fraction	freckles
frail	Fred
frame	free
Fran	freedom
France	freeway
frank	freeze
frantic	freezer
freak	freight

French	frisky
fresh	frizz
fret	frog
fried	from
friend	front
fright	frost
frighten	frosting
frigid	frown
frill	froze
fringe	fruit
frisk	fry

gr-

grab	grand
grace	grant
grade	grape
grandma	graph
grandpa	grasp
graft	grass
grain	grate
gram	gravy
gray	grim
graze	grime
grease	grin
great	grind
Greek	grits
green	groan
Greg	grocery
Greta	groom
grew	ground
grid	group
grill	gruff

pr-

praise	press
prance	pretend
prank	pretty
prawn	pretzel
pray	prey
prayer	price
preach	prick
present	pride
prime	prize
primp	problem
prince	prod
princess	prom
principal	prompt
print	proof
printer	proud
prior	prove
Priscilla	prowl
prism	prune
private	pry

tr-

trace	tram	tree	trio
track	trance	trek	trip
Tracy	trap	trend	triplet
trade	trash	Trent	troll
tragic	travel	trial	troop
trail	Travis	tribe	trot
train	tray	trick	trouble
trait	treat	tried	truck
		trim	true
		Trina	trunk
		trinket	try

st-

stack	stall	steak	sting
staff	stamp	steam	stink
stage	stand	steed	stir
stain	star	steep	stitch
stair	stare	steer	stock
stake	start	stem	stone
stale	state	step	stood
stalk	stay	stew	stool
		stick	story
		stiff	stove
		still	study

snack	snatch	snipe	snowfall
snag	sneak	snips	snowflake
snail	sneaky	snob	snowman
snake	sneer	snoop	snowplow
snap	sneeze	snooze	snowshoe
snapper	sniff	snore	snowstorm
snare	snip	snorkle	snowtire
snarl	snippet	snort	snowy
		snout	snub
		snow	snug
		snowball	snuggle

scab	scare	scoop	scrape
scald	scarecrow	scoot	scrapes
scale	scared	scorch	scratch
scalp	scarf	score	scream
scam	scarlet	Scott	screech
scan	scat	scour	screen
scar	school	scout	screw
scarce	scold	scowl	screwdriver
		scuff	script
		scram	scroll
		scrap	scrub

sp-

space	sponge
speak	spooky
spade	spool
special	spoon
Spain	sport
speck	spot
span	spouse
speed	spout
spar	spuds
spell	spun
spare	spy
Spencer	
spark	
spend	
spat	
spent	

spice
spider
spike
spill
spin
spinach
spine
spire
spoil
spoke
spoken

sw-

swab	swarm
swag	swat
swallow	sway
swam	sweat
swamp	sweaty
swampy	sweater
swan	Sweden
swap	sweep

sweet | swing
sweetest | swinging
swell | swirl
swept | swish
swift | switch
swifter | swivel
swim | swollen
swimmer | swoop
swimming | sword
swindle | swung
swine |

sk-

skate	skid
skateboard	skiing
skater	skill
skeleton	skillet
sketch	skillful
skew	skim
ski	skin
skiboot	skinny

skip
skipper
skirt
skit
skull
skunk
sky
skydiver
skydiving
skylight
skyscraper

sm-

smack	smelly
small	smile
smaller	smirk
smart	smite
smash	smitten
smear	smith
smell	smithy
smelt	smock

smog
smoke
smokehouse
smokestack
smoky
smolder
smooth
smother
smudge
smug
smuggle

tw–

twang	twine
twelve	twinge
twenty	twinkle
tweed	twirl
twice	twist
twiddle	twister
twig	twitch
twin	two

KE-804064 © Key Education • The Biggest Book of Reproducible Books • My Phonics Book   -95A-

str–

straight	strike
strain	string
strait	stripe
strange	stroke
stranger	stroll
strap	stroller
straw	strong
strawberry	stronger
stray	strongest
stream	structure
street	struggle
strength	stride
stress	
strict	
strictly	

KE-804064 © Key Education • The Biggest Book of Reproducible Books • My Phonics Book   -95-

wh-

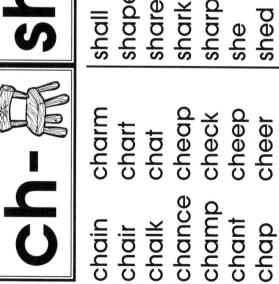

whale	which
wharf	while
what	whine
wheat	whirl
wheel	whisper
when	whistle
where	white
whether	why

th- "ȝ"

than	this
thank	three
that	threw
the	thrill
then	thought
they	those
thick	through
think	throw

ch-

chain	charm
chair	chart
chalk	chat
chance	cheap
champ	check
chant	cheep
chap	cheer
charge	cheese

sh-

shall	ship
shape	shirt
share	shoe
shark	shop
sharp	shook
she	short
shed	show
sheep	shut

-ch

arch
attach
beach
belch
coach
couch
each
rich
march
much
ouch
peach
such
teach
touch
which

-sh

bash
blush
brush
crush
dash
dish
finish
fish
foolish
fresh
hush
mash
push
rush
splash
trash

-th

bath
cloth
earth
faith
math
month
mouth
munch
north
path
Ruth
sixth
south
teeth
tooth

-nch

bench
crunch
drench
finch
inch
lunch
punch
ranch

-tch

batch
catch
clutch
fetch
hatch
itch
ditch
pitch

-ft

cleft	heft
craft	left
daft	lift
deft	raft
draft	rift
drift	shaft
gift	shift
graft	sift

swift
theft
thrift
tuft
waft

-ck

block	duck	pack	stick
brick	flock	peck	stock
chick	kick	pick	stuck
click	knock	pluck	tack
clock	lack	quack	thick
crack	luck	quick	track
deck	mock	rack	trick
dock	neck	rock	truck
		sick	whack
		slick	wick
		snack	wreck

-lf

elf
self
shelf
golf
gulf

-pt

crept
kept
rapt
slept
swept
wept

-mp

blimp	clump	jump	tamp
bump	cramp	lamp	scamp
camp	crimp	limp	skimp
champ	damp	lump	slump
chimp	dump	pomp	stamp
chomp	frump	plump	stomp
chump	grump	primp	stump
clamp	hump	pump	tramp
		ramp	thump
		romp	trump
		rump	

-lk

silk
stalk
sulk
talk
walk
yolk

balk
bilk
bulk
caulk
chalk
elk
hulk
milk

-lp

Help!

gulp
help
kelp
pulp
scalp
yelp

-ld

meld
mild
mold
old
scold
sold
told
wild

bald
bold
child
cold
fold
gold
held
hold

-lt

quilt
salt
smelt
stilt
tilt
volt
welt
wilt

belt
bolt
colt
dwelt
felt
gilt
halt
hilt

jilt
jolt
kilt
knelt
malt
melt
molt
pelt

-nd

sand
send
spend
stand
strand
tend
trend
vend
wend
wind

grind
hand
hind
kind
land
lend
mend
mind
pond
rend
rind

and
band
bend
bind
bland
blend
blind
blond

bond
brand
end
fend
find
fond
fund
gland

-nk

bank	drink	link	slink
blank	dunk	mink	stank
blink	flank	pink	stink
bunk	Frank	plank	stunk
clank	hank	prank	sunk
clink	honk	rink	tank
crank	junk	sank	thank
drank	kink	shank	think
		shrink	trunk
		sink	wink
		skunk	yank

-ng

bang	gang	ring	swing
bing	gong	sang	tang
bring	hang	sing	thing
clang	king	slang	tong
cling	long	sling	twang
ding	pang	song	wing
fang	ping	sprang	wring
fling	prong	spring	wrong
		sting	zing
		string	
		strong	

-ll

all
ball
bell
bill
call
chill
cell
dell

dill
doll
dwell
fall
fell
fill
full
hall

hill
ill
mall
mill
Nell
pall
pill
pull
sell
shell
small

smell
spill
squall
stall
swell
tall
tell
thrill
wall
well
yell

-nt

ant
bent
blunt
bunt
cent
dent
chant
gent

glint
grant
grunt
hint
hunt
Kent
lent
lint

mint
pant
plant
print
punt
rant
rent
runt
scant
scent
sent

slant
spent
splint
sprint
squint
stint
tent
tint
vent
went

-ff

bluff	huff	skiff
buff	miff	sluff
cuff	muff	sniff
chaff	off	snuff
cliff	puff	staff
fluff	quaff	stuff
gaff	ruff	tiff
gruff	scuff	whiff

-ss

bass	hiss	press
Bess	kiss	stress
bless	lass	Swiss
bliss	less	toss
boss	loss	tress
brass	mass	truss
chess	mess	
class	miss	
cross	moss	
floss	muss	
fuss	pass	
dress		
glass		
gloss		
grass		
guess		

-sk

whisk

ask
bask
brisk
brusk
cask
desk
disk
dusk

flask
frisk
husk
mask
risk
task
torsk
tusk

-zz

abuzz
buzz
fizz
frizz
fuzz
jazz
razz
pazazz

pizazz
whizz

-st

best	dust	just	quest
blast	fast	last	rest
blest	fist	lest	test
bust	frost	list	trust
cast	grist	lost	twist
chest	guest	mast	vast
cost	gust	mist	vest
crest	jest	must	west
		nest	wrest
		past	wrist
		pest	zest

-sp

asp	rasp
clasp	tieclasp
crisp	wasp
cusp	wisp
gasp	
grasp	
hasp	
lisp	

er

afternoon	dangerous
allergy	every
altered	federal
bakery	fern
battery	germ
boomerang	her
camera	herd
clerk	kernel

ladder
mother
nerve
offering
operate
over
perch
river
serve
sister
wonderful

ar

alarm	charm
arch	carp
ark	cart
arm	carve
art	chart
bark	dark
barn	darn
card	dart

farm
garden
hard
hark
harm
harp
large
lark
march
mark
market

park
part
party
shark
sharp
smart
star
starfish
start
warn
yard

ir 1st

affirm	circuit	girl	swirl
birch	confirm	girth	tapir
bird	dirt	irk	third
birth	dirty	shirk	thirst
birthday	fir	shirt	thirsty
chirp	firm	sir	thirteen
circle	first	skirt	thirty
circus	flirt	stir	twirl
		stirrup	Virginia
		squirm	whirl
		squirt	

or

acorn	fork	normal	sort
born	form	north	sport
chore	fort	orange	store
cord	horn	orbit	stork
cork	horse	orchard	storm
corn	more	porch	story
door	morn	pork	sword
for	morning	port	thorn
		shore	torch
		short	word
		sore	work

a_e

bake	frame	made	skate
brake	game	make	state
cake	gate	name	take
came	grade	plate	tale
cape	grape	rake	tame
crate	lake	sale	tape
date	late	same	trade
drape	lame	scrape	vase
		shade	wade
		shape	wake
		snake	whale

ur

burn	fur	nature	spur
burr	furniture	nurse	sure
burst	further	occur	surf
church	future	pleasure	surface
churn	hurry	purple	surprise
curb	hurt	purpose	Thursday
curl	hurry	purr	turkey
flurry	measure	purse	turn
		return	turtle
		scurry	urge
		slur	yogurt

KE-804064 © Key Education • The Biggest Book of Reproducible Books • My Phonics Book

KE-804064 © Key Education • The Biggest Book of Reproducible Books •

i_e

bike	drive	lime
bite	fine	line
chime	five	mime
chive	gripe	mite
crime	grime	nine
dime	hive	pipe
dine	kite	pine
dive	like	price
		ripe
		shine
		site

slide
slime
snipe
sprite
stripe
thrive
time
vine
white
wipe
write

e_e

Theme
Folder

scene
theme
these
eve
even

u_e

brute   flume   mute
chute   flute   plume
crude   fume   prude
cube   fuse   prune
cute   June   rude
dude   lute   rule
duke   mule   ruse
fluke   muse   tube
    tune
    yule

o_e

broke   drove   mope   scope
code   globe   nope   smoke
choke   grove   nose   spoke
chose   home   note   stove
close   hope   poke   stroke
coke   hose   probe   strode
cove   joke   quote   those
dome   lode   robe   vote
    rode   woke
    Rome   wrote
    rose   yoke

ay

away	gay	play
bay	gray	pray
bray	hay	quay
clay	jay	ray
cray	lay	say
crayon	may	slay
day	nay	spray
fray	pay	stay
		stray
		sway
		tray
		way
		x-ray

ai

afraid	detail	jail	rail
aim	explain	laid	rain
aid	fail	mail	remain
bait	faint	main	sail
braid	Gail	nail	snail
brain	hail	paid	sprain
chain	gain	pail	strait
claim	grain	pain	tail
		paint	trail
		plain	train
		quail	wait

ee

bee	leek
bleed	meek
deed	need
fee	peek
feed	preen
flee	queen
free	reed
freed	screen
glee	see
greed	seed
green	seek
heed	seem
jeep	seen
keep	sheep
knee	sleep
kneed	speed
	steed
	sweep
	tree
	tweed
	weed
	week

ea

beak	dream	mean
beam	eagle	meat
bean	eat	peak
bleak	freak	peal
clean	heal	real
creak	leak	scream
cream	lean	seal
deal	meal	seam
		sneak
		speak
		squeak

squeal
steal
streak
teak
teal
team
treat
veal
tweak
weak
zeal

oa

boast croak groan soak
boat float Joan soap
broach foal load throat
coast foam loan toad
cloak gloat moan toast
coach goad moat
coal goal poach
coat goat roach
      road
      roast
      roam

ow →

arrow glow slow
blow grow snow
borrow know snowball
bow low sow
bowl mow stow
crow own throw
flow row tomorrow
follow show tow
            yellow

au

August	caught
author	cause
autumn	caution
auto	dinosaur
autograph	daughter
autoharp	exhaust
Australia	faucet
because	fault

fraud
gauze
haul
jaunt
launch
haunt
laundry
naughty
sauce
sausage
vault

aw

awe	draw	lawn
awful	drawer	lawyer
awning	drawn	paw
bawl	fawn	pawn
caw	flaw	saw
claw	gnaw	scrawl
crawl	hawk	shawl
dawn	law	slaw
		squawk
		straw
		tawny

thaw
yawn

ow

allow	crowd	gown	shower
bow	crown	growl	somehow
brow	cowboy	how	sow
brown	down	howl	towel
chow	drown	now	tower
chowder	eyebrow	owl	town
clown	flower	plow	vow
cow	frown	powder	vowel
		power	
		prowl	
		scow	

ou

about	hound	our	scout
around	house	ourselves	shout
bound	loud	oust	sound
cloud	mouse	out	sour
couch	mouth	outdoors	south
count	mountain	outline	spout
found	ouch	outside	
ground	ounce	pouch	
		pound	
		proud	
		round	

oi

appoint
avoid
boil
broil
broiler
choice
coil
coin

doily
foil
join
joint
moist
moisture
noise
oil

oily
oink
point
poison
rejoice
sirloin
soil
spoil
toil
voice
void

oy

annoy
boy
boyhood
corduroy
cowboy
coy
destroy
employ

enjoy
joy
joyful
joyous
loyal
ploy
royal
soy

toy
Troy
voyage

oo

afoot	hood	notebook
book	hoof	overlook
brook	hook	shook
cook	look	soot
cookie	hood	stood
crook	nook	took
foot	rookie	understood
good	motherhood	wood
		wooden
		wool

oo

balloon	loose	shoot
bamboo	mood	smooth
bloom	moon	snoop
boo	noon	soon
boot	ooze	spoon
broom	pool	stoop
choose	roof	tool
cool	room	tooth
droop	school	troop
food	scoop	woo
fool	shampoo zoo	
gloom		
goose		
igloo		
kangaroo		
loop		

Y (ē)

any
baby
body
bossy
bumpy
copy
crunchy
daddy
early
easy
empty
every
funny
fussy
grumpy
happy

heavy
hilly
jelly
jellyfish
jolly
jumpy
many
merry
messy
mommy
money
muddy
only
plenty
pretty
quickly
ready
really
silly
tummy
ugly
very

Y (ī)

ally
apply
buy
by
bye
cry
cycle
defy
deny
dry
fry
hyena
my
myself
pry
reply

rye
shy
sky
sly
spy
style
try
why

My "All About Me" Book

This is me.

My "All About Me" Book Activity Suggestions

How to Make My "All About Me" Book: My "All About Me" Book (pages 120A–133A) is a fun book that the children can work on and add pages to all throughout the year. Copy the pages and cut along the dotted lines. Provide each child with a pocket folder to store all of their completed pages. When the books are finished, help the children punch two holes on the left side of each of the pages, and then bind the pages together using yarn or brads.

Getting Started

1. **Cover:** Begin this project by letting the children color their covers (page 120A) and tape photographs of themselves on the center of the star.

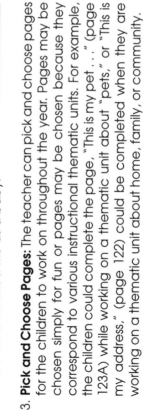

2. **Page 121:** Ask the children to bring to school baby pictures of themselves for the page "This is what I looked like as a baby."

3. **Pick and Choose Pages:** The teacher can pick and choose pages for the children to work on throughout the year. Pages may be chosen simply for fun or pages may be chosen because they correspond to various instructional thematic units. For example, the children could complete the page, "This is my pet . . ." (page 123A) while working on a thematic unit about "pets," or "This is my address," (page 122) could be completed when they are working on a thematic unit about home, family, or community.

4. **Adding Extra Pages:** Encourage the children to add pages of their own throughout the year. Page 133A may be used as a template for any additional topics.

This is where I live.

This is what I looked like as a baby.

This is my phone number

This is my address.

This is my pet . . .

or the animal I want as my pet.

This is my family.

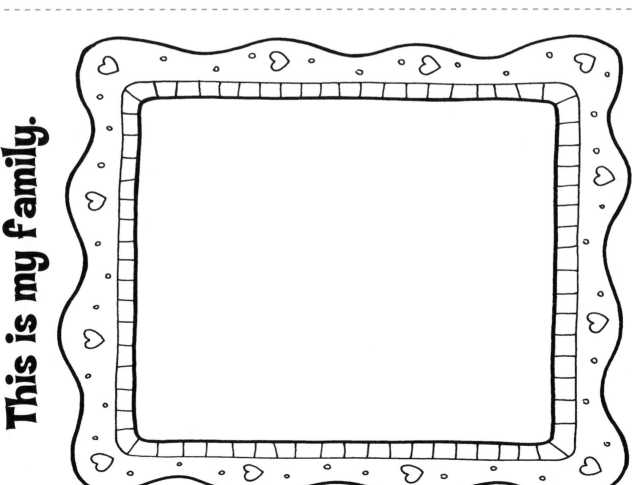

This is my teacher.

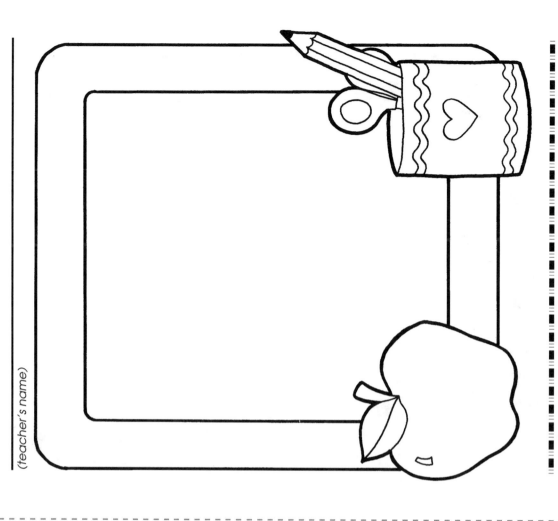

(teacher's name)

This is my school.

(name of school)

This is my favorite thing to do at home.

These are my friends.

(name of friend)

(name of school)

(name of friend)

(name of friend)

This is my favorite TV show.

(name of show)

This is my favorite toy.

(name of toy)

My Dream House

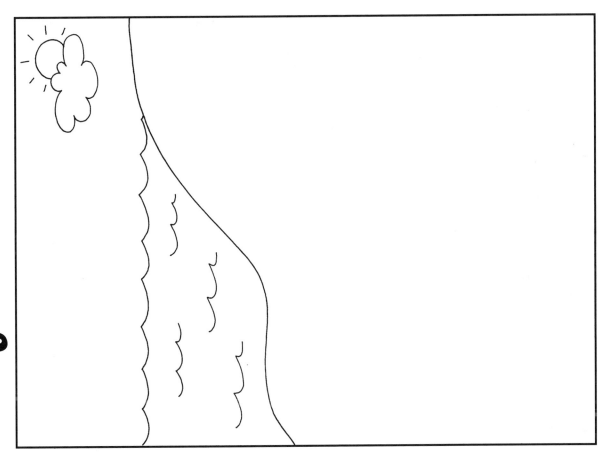

✂ -

10 things I like about me.

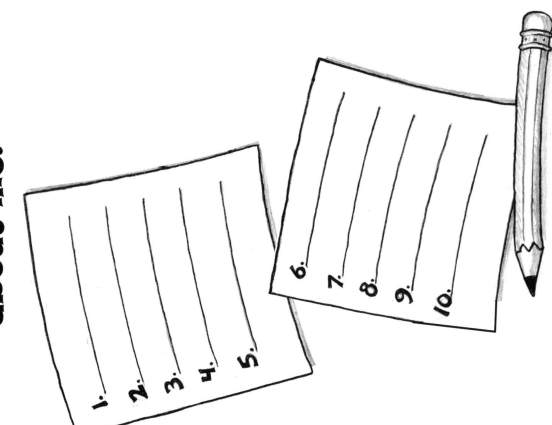

1.
2.
3.
4.
5.
6.
7.
8.
9.
10.

This is my favorite lunch.

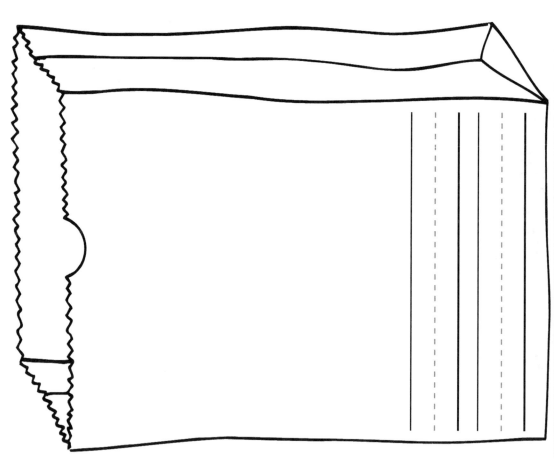

This is my favorite book.

The title is:

I want to win an award for:

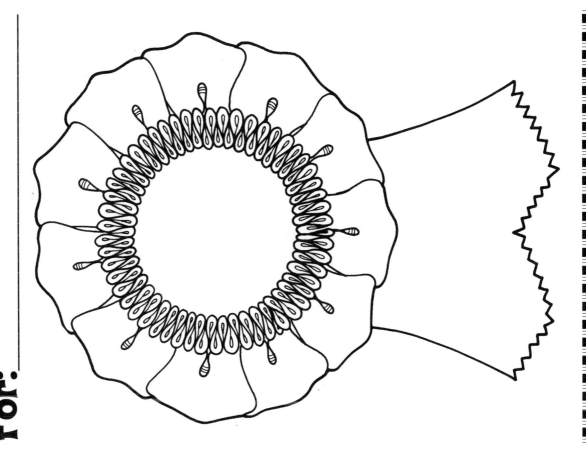

This is what I think you can see in outer space.

I am very good at . . .

✂

If I had one wish . . . I would wish for:

This is a picture of my greatest invention.

It is called a _____

My favorite song is:

_____
_____
_____
_____
_____

Here I am dancing and singing!

I am special because . . .

When I grow up I want to be . . .

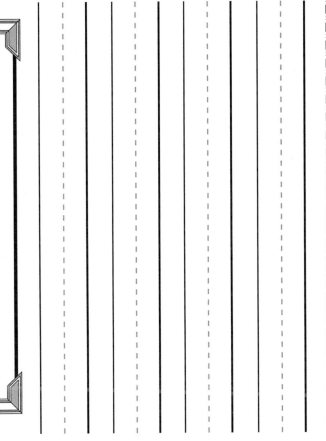

This is my favorite place.

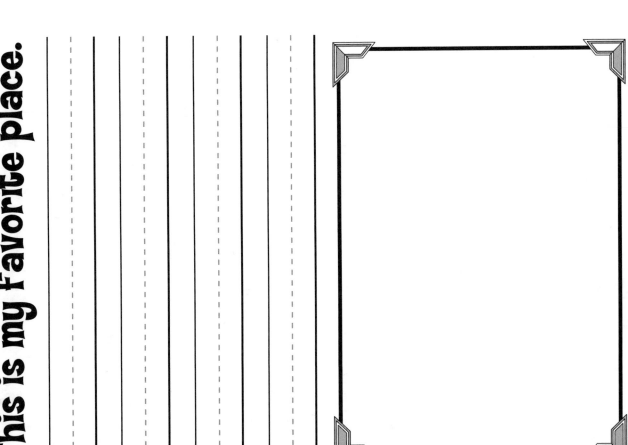

My Year Book

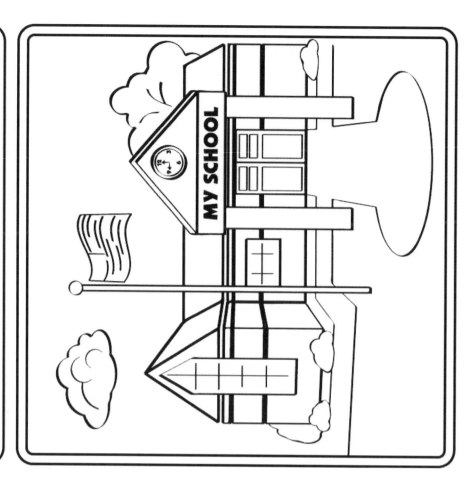

MY SCHOOL

Name _____

School Year _____

My Year Book
Activity Suggestions

How to Make My Year Book: My Year Book (pages 134A–143) is a fun book that helps children write about their school year memories, special events, friends, teachers, things they have learned, and how they have grown. This is another book that should be worked on all year long and will become a special memory book for each child.

Copy the pages and cut along the dotted lines. Provide each child with a pocket folder to store all their completed pages. When the books are finished, help the children punch two holes on the left side of the pages and then bind them together using yarn or brads.

Getting Started

1. **Cover:** Begin this project by letting the children color their covers (page 134A). You may also wish to "white out" the school illustration before copying so the children can place a photograph of their own school on the cover.

2. **We Went On Field Trips . . . and We Had Parties . . .:** We went on field trips . . . (page 136A) and We had parties . . . (page 136) should be completed after every field trip or party. Writing about school parties, field trips, and other special events right after they have happened make the writing experience much more valuable.

3. **Look How I Have Grown:** Page 140 should have the measurements recorded during the first week of school and during the last week of school. Children enjoying seeing how much they have grown.

4. **Pick and Choose Pages:** The teacher can pick and choose pages for the children to work on throughout the year.

5. **Autographs:** Make sure that the children have several of these pages. They will want to get everyone's autograph.

6. **Design Your Own Pages:** Encourage the children to add extra pages to their year books. Extra picture frames (page 144) and extra writing paper (page 144A) have been included for children to create their own pages. Here are some ideas for additional pages:

- School song
- Funniest Moment
- Favorite Substitute Teacher
- Classroom Cheer
- Classroom Visitors
- Our Principal
- The Best Joke
- Classroom Pet

This is my teacher.

My teacher's name is . . .

This is my school.

We had parties . . .

My favorite party was . . .

We went on field trips . . .

We went to . . .

Free-Time Fun!

During free time, I like to . . . .

These are my best friends.

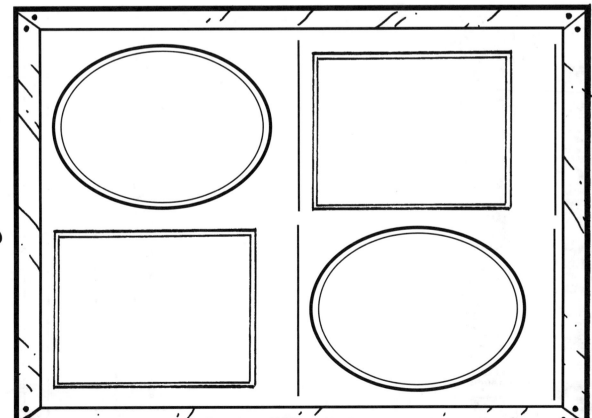

I learned a lot about ...

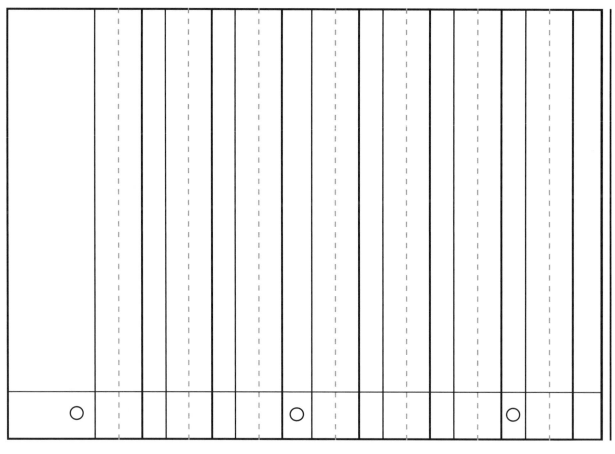

KE-804064 © Key Education • The Biggest Book of Reproducible Books • My School Year Book

My favorite subject is ...

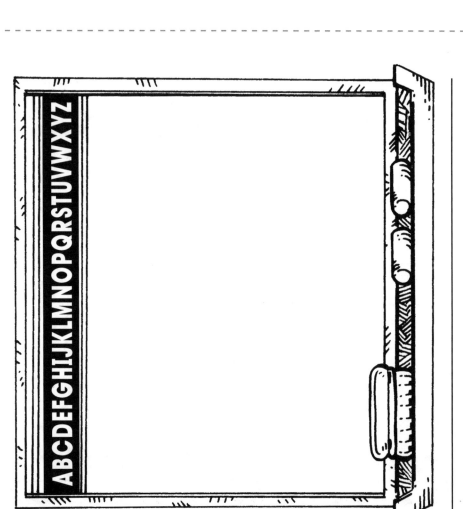

ABCDEFGHIJKLMNOPQRSTUVWXYZ

KE-804064 © Key Education • The Biggest Book of Reproducible Books • My School Year Book

My last day of school picture

Date:

My first day of school picture

Date:

This made me laugh . . .

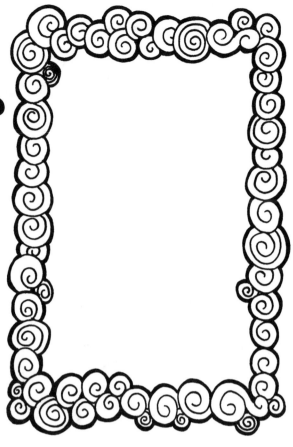

This is what happened . . .

_____

_____

_____

_____

Look at how I have grown!

How tall was I?

First of the year   End of the year

How much did I weigh?

First of the year   End of the year

4

3

2

1

0

My teacher read the best story…

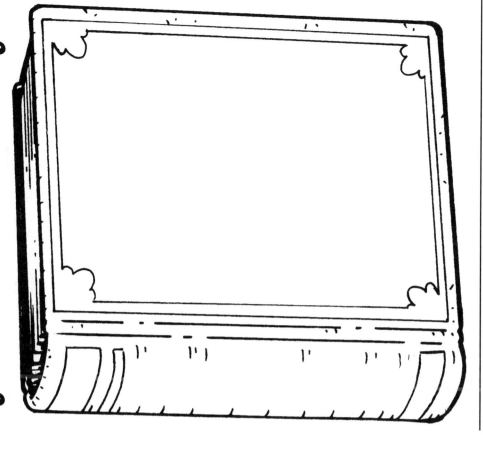

KE-804064 © Key Education • The Biggest Book of Reproducible Books • My School Year Book

My favorite school song is…

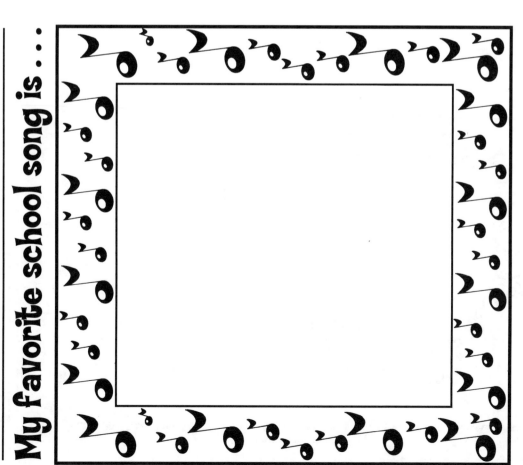

KE-804064 © Key Education • The Biggest Book of Reproducible Books • My School Year Book

My favorite people at school are . . .

I should get an award for . . .

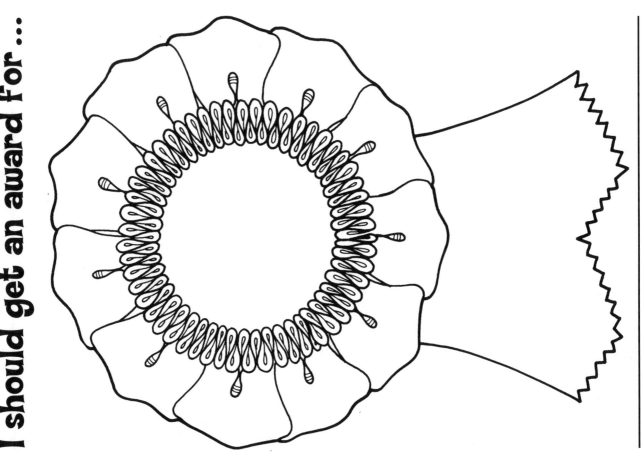

Autographs of my friends!

On the last day of school I . . . .

(extra writing paper)

Extra Frames

My Own Newspaper – Activity Suggestions

How to Make My Own Newspaper: My Own Newspaper templates can be found on pages 146 and 147. Young children benefit from learning about print in their world. They should be encouraged to read magazines, maps, menus, phone directories, catalogs, books, and newspapers. Reading or listening to short newspaper articles can help to improve comprehension and help children learn more of what is happening in the world around them.

Create a Classroom Newspaper

1. **Name your newspaper:** Let the students vote on a name.

2. **Sections of My Own Newspaper:** Identify the different sections of a newspaper that you would like to include in your classroom newspaper, such as news articles, feature stories, comics, advertisements, sports, and riddles and jokes.

3. **Brainstorm Story Ideas:** Brainstorm ideas for possible articles and have the students select what they would like to write about. Also brainstorm questions that the students should ask when researching and preparing to write the newspaper articles.

4. **Peer Feedback:** Organize your classroom by using the principles of a writers workshop. This will ensure that the students are sharing what they are working on with other students while also getting feedback from their classmates.

5. **Final Pages:** Once the students have finished their individual assignments they should write their final drafts on copies of the newspaper template. The teacher can then copy all of the pages. Have the students collate the pages and staple them together.

6. **Newspaper Delivery:** Have the students pass out their newspaper to other classrooms, the principal, and to other school staff members. Make sure each student brings home a copy as well.

Graphic Novels (Comic Strips) – Activity Suggestions

How to Use the Graphic Novel Templates: The graphic novel templates (or more commonly known as comic strips) are found on pages 148–151. Comic strips, for many reasons, are wonderful tools for teaching reading and writing skills. First, comic strips are motivational and child-friendly—they simply appeal to children. Comic strip characters and story plots are often funny, colorful, and are usually topics that children are interested in and can understand. Next, comic strips can be used successfully with all ability levels. Children who are good readers and writers, as well as children who are struggling with literacy skills, can use comic strip formats effectively.

- **Page 148:** 4 boxes with speech bubbles. This is a good template for a two person conversation that includes a beginning, middle, and ending.

- **Page 149:** 6 boxes that include backgrounds and a narration box. This is a good comic strip for writing a story through the voice of a narrator.

- **Page 150:** 6 boxes with speech bubbles. This is a good template for a more complicated two person conversation.

- **Page 151:** This is a 9-panel filmstrip.

- **Add extra pages:** Every template can become an extended graphic novel by adding pages.

Graphic Novels Springboard Ideas:

- **Cut-Apart Real Comic Strips:** Find some real (and appropriate) comic strips in local newspapers. Let the children read the comics. Then cut the comic strip boxes apart and have the children put them back together in the correct story sequence.

- **Comic Book Teams:** Let the children work in pairs or teams. They can decide together on a story plot and write the conversation for a specific character.

- **Other:** Comic strips are great for teaching how to use quotation marks, for answering who, what, when, where, and why questions, writing dialogue, and to see how important illustrations are to understanding content.

MY OWN NEWSPAPER

Date:

_____

story title

illustration

story title

illustration

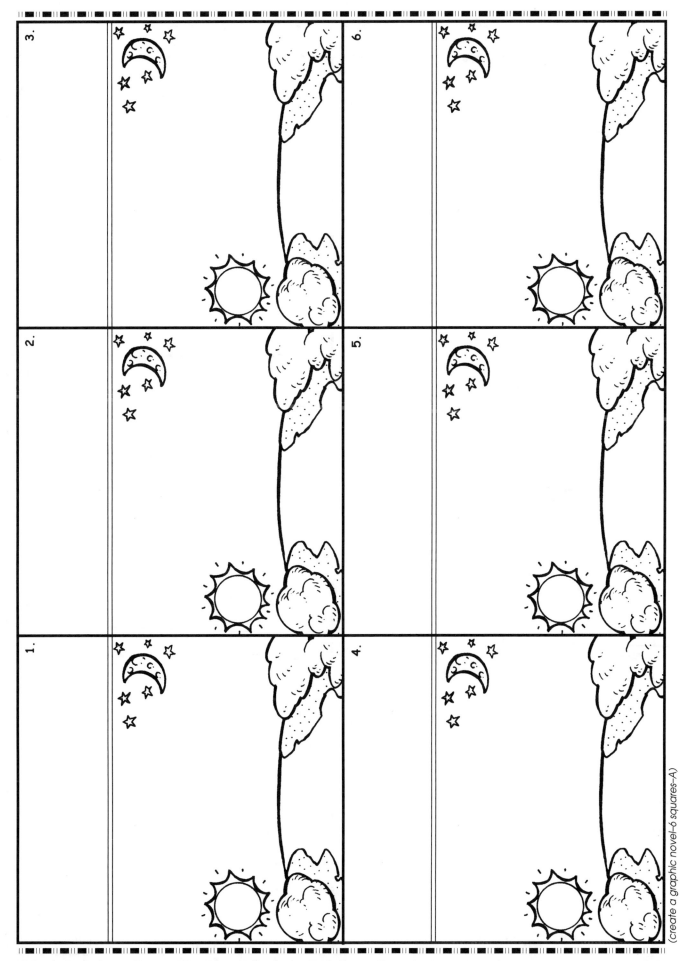

(create a graphic novel–6 squares–A)

(create a filmstrip)

Accordion Book

How to Make an Accordion Book: Accordion Books are great fun to make and they allow the writer to decide "how long" or "how short" to make their story. You may choose to use the reproducible patterns provided on this page and page 153, or you can follow these directions to make a simple accordion book from lined writing paper and construction paper.

1. Tape several sheets of lined writing paper together as shown.
2. Using construction paper, add both a front and back cover. (See illustration.)

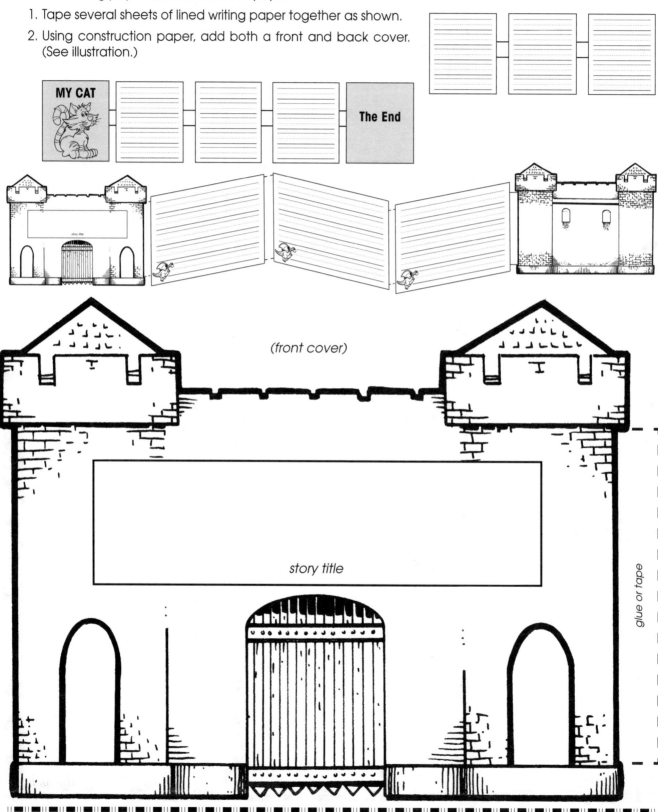

(front cover)

story title

glue or tape

(accordion book inside pages)

glue or tape

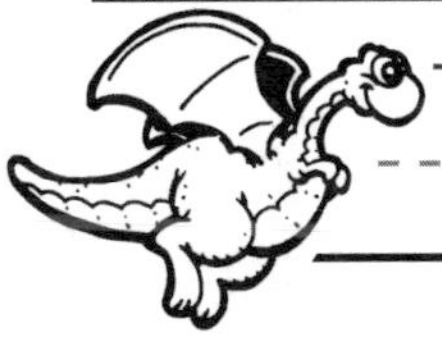

glue or tape

(back cover)

glue or tape

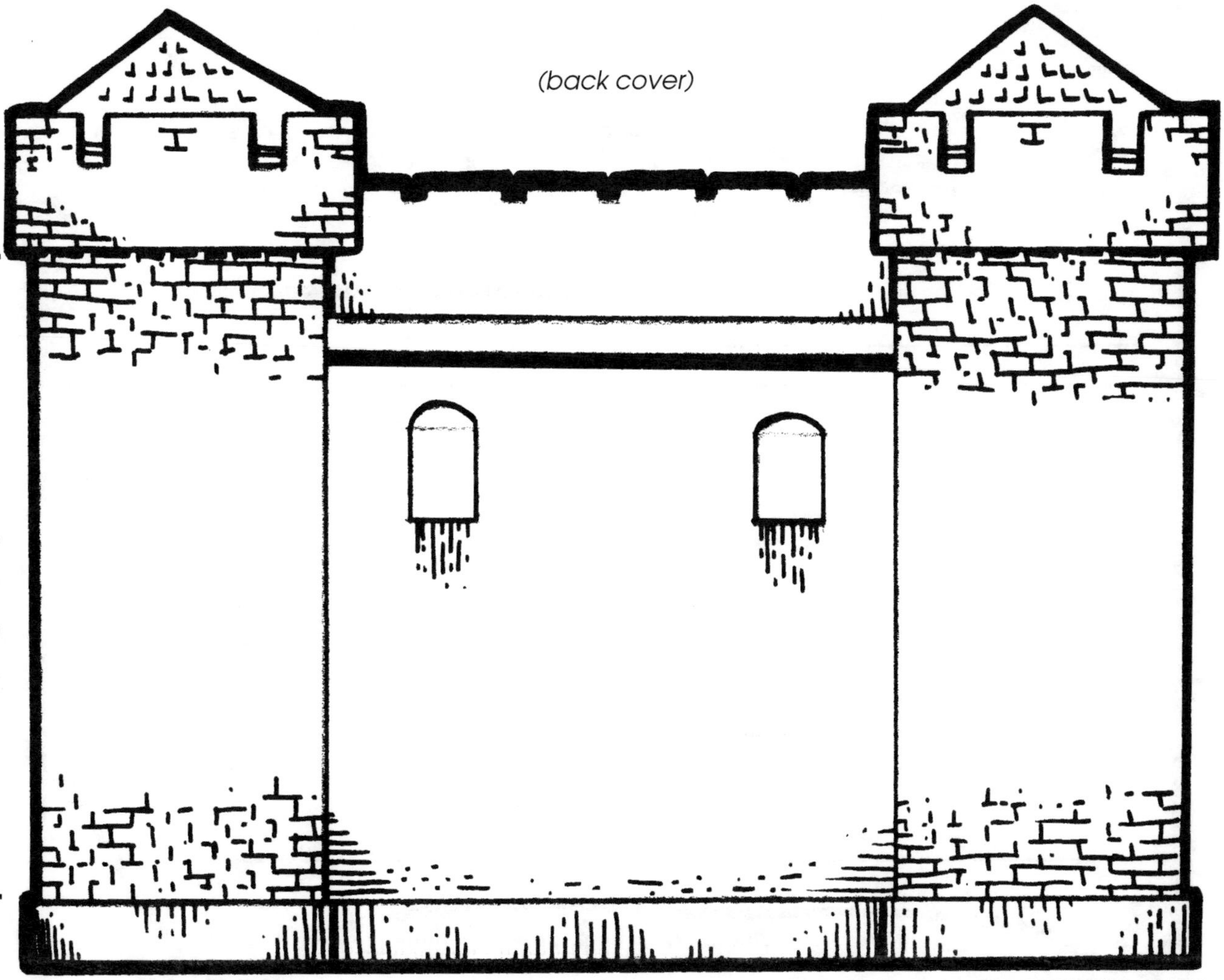

story title

Shape Book Directions: The shape books are found on pages 154–159. Copy the cover and as many pages as needed for the child's story. Staple together when complete.

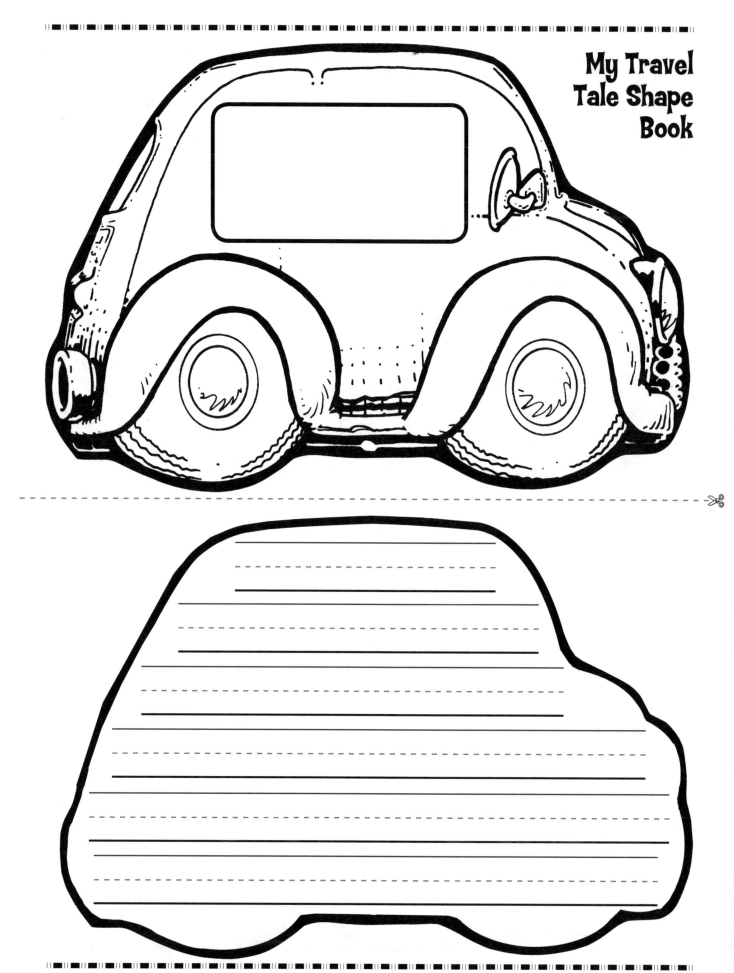

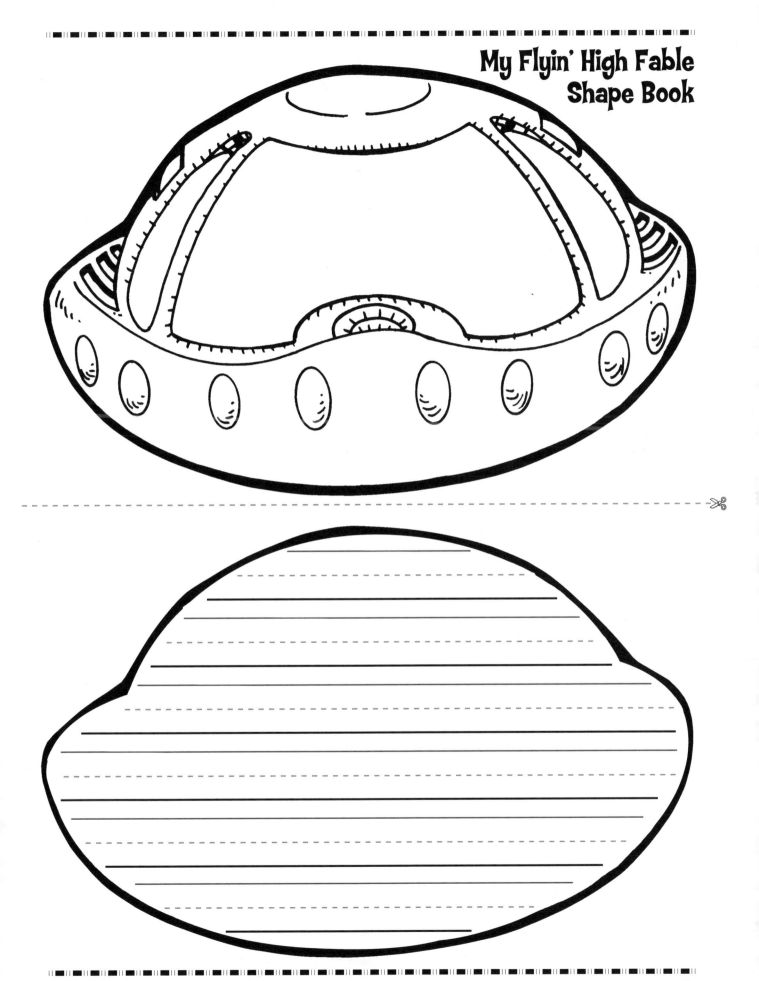

Notes